# Thunder and Lightning

## by Grace Hansen

Abdo
**WEATHER**
Kids

**abdopublishing.com**

Published by Abdo Kids, a division of ABDO, PO Box 398166, Minneapolis, Minnesota 55439.

Printed in the United States of America, North Mankato, Minnesota.

052015

092015

 THIS BOOK CONTAINS
RECYCLED MATERIALS

Photo Credits: iStock, Shutterstock, © Versageek / CC-SA-3.0 p.5

Production Contributors: Teddy Borth, Jennie Forsberg, Grace Hansen

Design Contributors: Laura Rask, Dorothy Toth

Library of Congress Control Number: 2014958419

Cataloging-in-Publication Data

Hansen, Grace.

 Thunder and lightning / Grace Hansen.

  p. cm. -- (Weather)

ISBN 978-1-62970-934-5

Includes index.

1. Thunder--Juvenile literature.   2. Lightning--Juvenile literature.   I. Title.

551--dc23

                2014958419

# Table of Contents

## Thunderclouds

Thunderclouds are dark. They always make thunder and lightning. Sometimes they make hail. They can make tornadoes, too.

Water droplets are inside a thundercloud. There are also ice crystals inside. It is very windy inside the cloud.

7

The wind moves everything around. The water droplets crash into each other. This makes **static electricity**. An electric charge builds up.

9

The charge gets very powerful.

It looks for a way to **escape**.

10

11

# Lightning

The charge **escapes** as lightning. Lightning can happen between clouds. Or it can happen inside a cloud. Lightning also travels from a cloud to the ground.

13

The electric charge tries to find the easiest path downward. The **stepped leader** finds the path. We see this as lightning.

15

The air around the lightning gets very hot. This very hot air **expands** quickly.

## Thunder

The **expanding** air **vibrates**.
It makes a rumbling or cracking
noise. This sound is thunder.

19

Light travels faster than sound.

We always see lightning before

we hear thunder.

We see **LIGHTNING** .oooooo5 seconds after lightning strikes one mile away

We hear **THUNDER** 5 seconds after lightning strikes one mile away

**O** seconds   **1** second   **2** seconds   **3** seconds   **4** seconds   **5** seconds

21

# How Lightning Forms

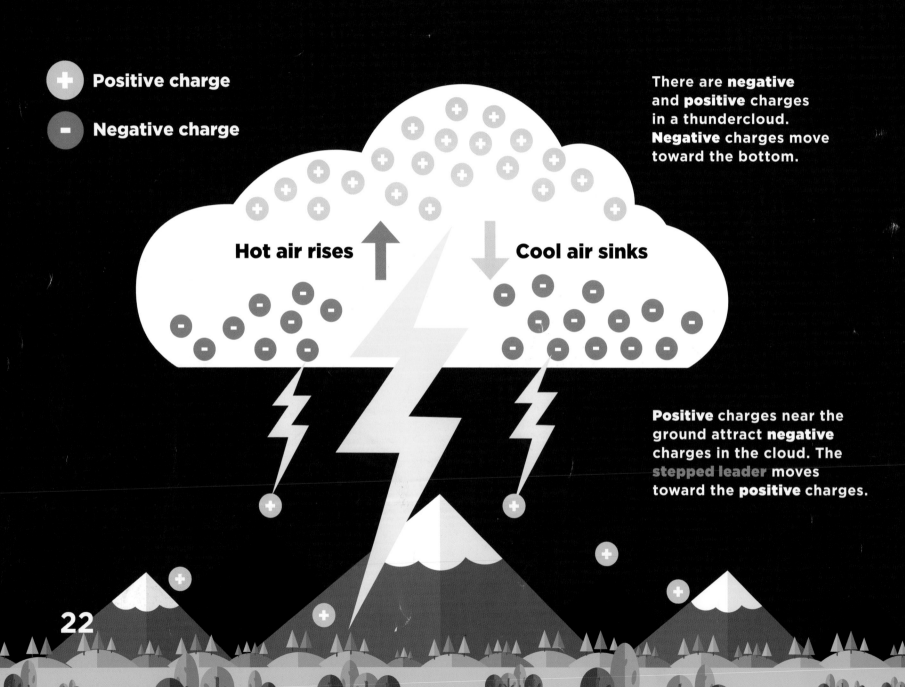

- ➕ **Positive charge**
- ➖ **Negative charge**

There are **negative** and **positive** charges in a thundercloud. **Negative** charges move toward the bottom.

Hot air rises ⬆ ⬇ Cool air sinks

**Positive** charges near the ground attract **negative** charges in the cloud. The **stepped leader** moves toward the **positive** charges.

# Glossary

**escape** – to get free of.

**expand** – to spread out.

**static electricity** – a stationary electric charge, usually produced by friction, that causes sparks or crackling or the attraction of dust or hair.

**stepped leader** – the way negative electrical charges in the cloud find positive charges near the ground. Leaders work their way downward in quick steps. This is why lightning does not look straight.

**vibrate** – to move back and forth very quickly.

# Index

## abdokids.com

Use this code to log on to abdokids.com and access crafts, games, videos, and more!

Abdo Kids Code:
WTK9345